CONTRACEPTION AND CHASTITY

by
Elizabeth Anscombe

*All booklets are published thanks to the
generous support of the members of the
Catholic Truth Society*

CATHOLIC TRUTH SOCIETY
PUBLISHERS TO THE HOLY SEE

2

CONTENTS

FOREWORD

Contraception and Chastity, based on a talk given by Elizabeth Anscombe some years previously, was first published in pamphlet form in 1975. Its author was a Catholic convert, and the mother of seven children. She was also a famous philosopher, particularly distinguished for her work on the topic of intention.*

The thoughts which she expresses in this pamphlet were worked out (mostly before the appearance of *Humanae Vitae*) at that crossroads in the history of the Church, when it appeared to some Catholics that it might be possible, and consistent with Catholic teaching about marriage, to allow the use of contraceptives by married couples, and that this would not lead to a general abandonment of teaching about fornication, sodomy, base methods of copulation, and other sins against chastity.

As Anscombe argues, to accept contraception is, if we reason it through, to leave ourselves with no clear

---

* She had found that fellow philosophers at Oxford were ignorant about this subject: they argued that, in itself, the action of a man who ordered the bombing of a city was only to sign his name on a piece of paper. As a Catholic she had been taught better. She therefore gave a course of lectures which became a book, *Intention* [1957], a ground-breaking work which opened up for analytic philosophers the field they now call 'action theory'.

and compelling reason for avoiding personal unchastity. She does not enlarge on the wider bearings and implications of the Church's teaching about marriage, but restricts herself to the minimum which makes of that teaching a consistent whole, and points to the effect on people's lives of not accepting that minimum. She also sets forth, briefly, the historic roots and development of the doctrine.

The advantage of this uncluttered exposition is that it enables her to distinguish sharply between contraceptive behaviour and the use of the rhythm method. Some people think that the basis of this distinction has to do with certainty of effect, but of course modern natural family planning methods can give better control over conception than, say, the use of condoms.

It is about this distinction that her expertise on the subject of intention comes into play. Her argument here deserves very close attention, bearing in mind the fact which she points out: that every sexual act is significant. This means that the question of whether an individual act of intercourse is a chaste one is as important as the question of whether the marriage as a whole is open to life.

As a writer, Anscombe was terse and unrepetitive. If you try to read quickly through this pamphlet you may miss something important. At the request of the publishers I have added subheadings to the text which are intended to make this less likely.

Elizabeth Anscombe upheld the teaching of Pope Paul VI but the thinking that enabled her to welcome *Humanae Vitae* when it came out was based on her own firm faith in the truth of Catholic tradition.

Mary C Gormally

I. THE CHURCH, THE WORLD AND CHASTITY

A new set of circumstances ...

I will first ask you to contemplate a familiar point: the fantastic change that has come about in people's situation in respect of having children because of the invention of efficient contraceptives. You see, what can't be otherwise we accept; and so we accept death and its unhappiness. But possibility destroys mere acceptance. And so it is with the possibility of having intercourse and preventing conception. This power is now placed in a woman's hands; she needn't have children when she doesn't want to and she can still have her man! This can make the former state of things look intolerable, so that one wonders why they were so pleased about weddings in former times and why the wedding day was supposed to be such a fine day for the bride.

... but there is nothing new in the division between Church and world ...

There always used to be a colossal strain in ancient times between heathen morality and Christian morality, and one of the things pagan converts had to be told about the way they were entering on was that they must abstain from fornication. This peculiarity of the Christian life was taught in a precept issued by the Council of Jerusalem, the very first council of the Christian Church. The prohibition was issued in the same breath as the merely temporary retention of Judaic laws prohibiting the eating of blood - no black pudding! - and the prohibition on eating the flesh of animals that had been sacrificed to idols. And in one way these may have been psychologically the same sort of prohibition to a pagan convert. The Christian life simply imposed these peculiar restrictions on you. All the same the prohibition on fornication must have stood out; it must have meant a very serious change of life to many, as it would today. Christian life meant a separation from the standards of that world: you couldn't be a Baal-worshipper, you couldn't sacrifice to idols, be a sodomite, practice infanticide, compatibly with the Christian allegiance. That is not to say that Christians were good; we humans are a bad lot and our lives as Christians even if not blackly and grossly wicked are usually very mediocre. But the Catholic Christian badge now again means separation, even for such poor mediocrities, from what the unchristian world in the West approves and professes.

... especially about marriage ...

Christianity was at odds with the heathen world, not only about fornication, infanticide and idolatry; but also about marriage. Christians were taught that husband and wife had equal rights in one another's bodies; a wife is *wronged* by her husband's adultery as well as a husband by his wife's. And Christianity involved non-acceptance of the contemptible role of the female partner in fornication, calling the prostitute to repentance and repudiating respectable concubinage. And finally for Christians divorce was excluded. These differences *were* the measure, great enough, of the separation between Christianity and the pagan world in these matters. By now, Christian teaching is, of course, *known* all over the world; and it goes without saying for those in the West that what they call "accepting traditional morals" means counting fornication as wrong - it's just not a respectable thing. But we ought to be conscious that, like the objection to infanticide, this is a Jewish-Christian inheritance. And we should realise that heathen humanity tends to have a different attitude towards both. In Christian teaching a value is set on every human life and on men's chastity as well as on women's and this as part of the ordinary calling of a Christian, not just in connexion with the austerity of monks. Faithfulness, by which a man turned only to his spouse, forswearing all other women, was counted as one of *the* great goods of marriage.

... though now the rift is wider

But the quarrel is far greater between Christianity and the present-day heathen, post-Christian, morality that has sprung up as a result of contraception. In one word: Christianity taught that men ought to be as chaste as pagans thought honest women ought to be; the contraceptive morality teaches that women need to be as little chaste as pagans thought men need be.

The contraceptive mentality
opposed to the ideal of chastity

And if there is nothing intrinsically wrong with contraceptive intercourse, and if it could become general practice everywhere when there is intercourse but ought to be no begetting, then it's very difficult to see the objection to this morality; for the ground of objection to fornication and adultery was that sexual intercourse is only right in the *sort* of set-up that typically provides children with a father and mother to care for them. If you can turn intercourse into something other than the reproductive type of act (I don't mean of course that every act is reproductive any more than every acorn leads to an oak tree but it's the reproductive *type* of act) then why, if you can change it, should it be restricted to the married? Restricted, that is, to partners bound in a formal, legal, union whose fundamental purpose is the bringing up of children? For if that is not its fundamental purpose there is no reason why for example "marriage" should have to be between people of opposite sexes. But then, of course, it becomes unclear why you should have a ceremony, why you should have a formality at all. And so we must grant that children are in this general way the main point of the existence of such an arrangement. But if sexual union can be deliberately and totally divorced from fertility, then we may wonder why sexual union has got to be married union. If the expression of love between the partners is the point, then it shouldn't be so narrowly confined.

The only objection, then, to the new heathen, contraceptive morality will be that the second condition I mentioned - near-universality of contraception where there ought not to be begetting - simply won't be fulfilled. Against the background of a society with that morality, more and more people will have intercourse with little feeling of responsibility, little restraint, and *yet* they just won't be so careful about always using contraceptives. And so the widespread use of contraceptives naturally leads to more and more rather than less and less abortion.[1] Indeed, abortion is now being recommended as a population control measure - a second line of defence.

Now if this - that you won't get this universal "taking care" - is the only objection then it's a pretty miserable outlook. Because, like the fear of venereal disease, it's an objection that's little capable of moving people or inspiring them as a positive ideal of chastity may.

---

[1] The exception to this in the short term is where abortion has been encouraged and contraceptives not available; making contraceptives available then produces an immediate but only temporary reduction in abortions.

Two senses of the word chastity

The Christian Church has taught such an ideal of chastity: in a narrower sense, and in a broader sense in which chastity is simply the virtue whose topic is sex, just as courage is the virtue whose topic is danger and difficulty. In the narrower sense chastity means continence, abstention. I have to say something about this - though I'm reduced to stammering because I am a mediocre worldly person leading an ordinary sort of worldly life; nevertheless I'll try to say it even with stammering.

The ideal of celibacy

What people are for is, we believe, like guided missiles, to home in on God, God who is the one truth it is infinitely worth knowing, the possession of which you could never get tired of, like the water which if you have you can never thirst again, because your thirst is slaked forever and always. It's this potentiality, this incredible possibility, of the knowledge of God of such a kind as even to be sharing in his nature, which Christianity holds out to people; and because of this potentiality every life, right up to the last, must be treated as precious. Its potentialities in all things the world cares about may be slight; but there is always the possibility of what it's for. We can't ever know that the time of possibility of gaining eternal life is over, however old, wretched, "useless" someone has become.

Now there are some people who want this so much that they want to be totally concerned with it and to die to their own worldly, earthly and fleshly desires. It is people who are so filled with this enormous desire and are able to follow it, who pursue the course of chastity in the narrow sense - this is the point, the glory, of Christian celibacy and virginity and of vows of chastity. I think one has to know about it in order to appreciate the teachings of Christianity about chastity in a wide sense. But as I say I speak stammeringly because I'm not very well qualified.

II. Discussion of the Historic Teaching on Contraception as an Offence Against Chastity in the Broader Sense

The early Church

Turning to chastity not in the narrower sense but in the sense in which it is simply the virtue connected with sex, the Christian Church has always set its face against contraception from the earliest time as a grave breach of chastity. It inherited from Israel the objection to "base ways of copulating for the avoidance of conception", to quote St Augustine. In a document of the third century a Christian author wrote of the use of contraceptives by freeborn Christian women of Rome. These women sometimes married slaves so as to have Christian husbands but they were under a severe temptation because if the father was a slave the child was a slave by Roman law and this was a deterrent to having children; and they practised some form of contraception. This was the occasion of the earliest recorded explicit Christian observation on the subject. The author writes like a person mentioning a practice which Christians at large must obviously regard as shameful.

Augustine and the Manichaeans

From then on the received teaching of Christianity has been constant. We need only mention two landmarks which have stood as signposts in Christian teaching - the teaching of Augustine and that of Thomas Aquinas. St Augustine wrote against the Manichaeans. The Manichaeans were people who thought all sex evil. They thought procreation was worse than sex; so if one must have sex let it be without procreation which imprisoned a soul in flesh. So they first aimed to restrict intercourse altogether to what they thought were infertile times and also to use contraceptive drugs so as if possible never to have children. If they did conceive they used drugs to procure abortions; finally, if that failed, in their cruel lust or lustful cruelty, as St Augustine says, they might put the child out to die. (The appetite for killing children is a rather common characteristic in the human race.)

All these actions Augustine condemned and he argued strongly against their teaching. Sex couldn't possibly be evil; it is the source of human society and life is God's good creation. On the other hand it is a familiar point that there is some grimness in Augustine's view of sex. He regards it as more corrupted by the fall than our other faculties. Intercourse for the sake of getting children is good but the need for sexual intercourse otherwise, he thought, is an infirmity. However, "husband and wife" (I quote) "owe one another not only the faithful association of sexual union for the sake of getting children - which makes the first society of the human race in this our mortality - but more than that a kind of mutual service of bearing the burden of one another's weakness, so as to prevent unlawful intercourse."

Augustine holds up as an ideal something which he must have known didn't happen all that much: the life of married people who no longer seeking children are able to live in continence. He considers it a weakness that few ever do this. There's a sort of servitude to fleshly desire in not being able so to abstain. But marriage is so great a good, he said, that it altogether takes vice out of this; and what's bad about our weakness is thereby excused. If one partner demands sexual intercourse out of the pressure of sexual desire, he says, the other does right in according it. But there is at least venial sin in demanding it from this motive, and if one's very intemperate, mortal sin.

Intercourse purely for pleasure sinful even in marriage

All this part of his teaching is very uncongenial to our time. But we must notice that it has been a bit misrepresented. It has been said that for Augustine sexual intercourse not for the sake of getting children involves actual sin, though not mortal sin - a little bit of sin - on the part of at least one partner, the partner who demands it. What he seems to say however is not that, but something different; that if one seeks it out of mere fleshly desire for the sake of pleasure, there is such sin; and this latter teaching has in fact been constant among all the saints and doctors of the Church who have written on the matter at all. (I will be coming back to this.)

The marriage debt

St Augustine indeed didn't write explicitly of any other motive than mere sensuality in seeking intercourse where procreation isn't aimed at. What he says doesn't exclude the possibility of a different motive. There's the germ of an account of the motive called by theologians "rendering the marriage debt" in his observation that married people owe to one another a kind of mutual service. Aquinas made two contributions, the first of which concerns this point: he makes the remark that a man ought to pay the marriage debt if he can see his wife wants it without her having to ask him. And he ought to notice if she does want it. This is an apt gloss on Augustine's "mutual service", and it destroys the basis for the picture which some have had of intercourse not for the sake of children as necessarily a little bit sinful on one side, since one must be "demanding", and not for any worthy motive but purely "out of desire for pleasure". One could hardly say that being diagnosable as wanting intercourse was a sin! St Thomas, of course, speaks of the matter rather from the man's side, but the same thing could be said from the woman's, too; the only difference being that her role would be more that of encouragement and invitation. (It's somewhat modern to make this comment. We are much more conscious nowadays of people's complexities and hang-ups than earlier writers seem to have been.)

St Thomas follows St Augustine and all other traditional teachers in holding that intercourse sought out of lust, only for the sake of pleasure, is sin, though it is venial if the intemperance isn't great, and in type this is the least of the sins against chastity.

'Sins against nature'
- a technical term for perverse sex acts

His second contribution was his definition of the "sin against nature". This phrase relates to deviant acts, such as sodomy and bestiality. He defined this type of sin as a sexual act of such a kind as to be intrinsically unfit for generation. This definition has been colossally important. It was, indeed, perfectly in line with St Augustine's reference to copulating in a "base" way so as not to procreate, thus to identify some ways of contraception practised in former times as forms of unnatural vice. For they would, most of them, be deviant sexual acts.

Medical methods seen as homicidal

Contraception by medical methods, however, as well as abortion, had previously been characterised as homicide throughout the dark ages. And this seems a monstrously unreasonable stretching of the idea of homicide. Not unreasonable in the case of abortion; though some may doubt (it's a rather academic question, I think, an intensely academic question) the good sense of calling a fertilised ovum a human being. But soon there is something of a human shape; and anyway this is the definite beginning of a human being (or beings in the case of a split - where you get twins - the split occurs soon, at least within two weeks), and if you perform an abortion at that early stage all the same you are destroying that human beginning.

But of course the notion of homicide is just not extendable to most forms of contraception. The reason why it seemed to be so in the dark ages (by the "dark ages" I mean roughly from the 4th-5th centuries on to the 12th, say - I won't make an apology for using the expression - scientifically it was pretty dark) was that it was taken for granted that medical methods were all abortifacient in type. We have to remember that no one knew about the ovum. Then, and in more primitive times, as language itself reveals with its talk of "seed", the woman's body was thought of as being like the ground in which seed was planted. And thus the perishing of the seed once planted would be judged by people of those times to be the same sort of event as we would judge the perishing of a fertilised ovum to be and hence the deliberate bringing about of the one would be just like the deliberate bringing about of the other. So that is the explanation of the curiosity that historically medical contraception was equated with homicide - it was equated with homicide because they thought it was that sort of thing, the sort of thing that destroying a fertilised ovum is.[2]

When Aristotle's philosophy became dominant in the thirteenth century a new (but still erroneous) picture replaced that ancient one: namely that the woman provided the *matter,* and the man the formative principle of a new conception. This already made that extended notion of "homicide" look untenable - contraception that would prevent the formation would obviously not be destroying something that was already the beginning of new human life. With modern physiological knowledge contraception by medical methods could be clearly distinguished from early abortion, though some contraceptive methods might be abortifacient.

Can contraception be seen as perversion?
An intellectual problem

On the other hand intercourse using contraception by mechanical methods was fairly easy to assimilate to the "sin against nature" as defined by St Thomas. Looking at it like this is aided by the following consideration: suppose that somebody's contraceptive method were to adopt some clearly perverse mode of copulation, one

---

[2] Indeed some contraceptive drugs do tend to have an abortifacient effect by preventing implantation. *[Ed.]*

wouldn't want to say he committed two distinct sins, one of perversion and the other of contraception: there'd be just the one evil deed, precisely because the perversity of the mode consists in the physical act being changed so as to be not the sort of act that gets a child at all.

And so the theologians tried to extend the notion of the evil as one of perversity - speaking, for example, of the "perverse use of a faculty" - so as to cover all types of contraception including medical ones which after all don't change the mere physical act into one of the type: "sin against nature".

For with contraception becoming common in this country and the Protestants approving it in the end, the Popes reiterated the condemnation of it. It was clear that the condemnation was of deliberately contraceptive intercourse as a breach of chastity, as "a shameful thing". But the rationale offered by the theologians was not satisfactory. The situation was intellectually extremely distressing. On the one hand, it would have been absurd, wouldn't it? to approve douches, say, while forbidding condoms. On the other hand, the extension of the notion of a perverse act, a deviant act, seemed strained.

Furthermore, while one doesn't *have* to be learned (nobody has to be learned) or able to give a convincing account of the reasons for a teaching - for remember that the Church teaches with the authority of a divine commission, and the Pope has a prophetical office, not a chair of science or moral philosophy or theology - all the same the moral teaching of the Church, by her own claims, is supposed to be reasonable. Christian moral teachings aren't revealed mysteries like the Trinity. The lack of clear accounts of the reason in the teaching was disturbing to many people. Especially, I believe, to many of the clergy whose job it was to give the teaching to the people.

The twentieth century Church and Catholic families

Again, with effective contraceptive techniques and real physiological knowledge available, a new question came to the fore. I mean that of the rational limitation of families. Because of ignorance, people in former times who did not choose continence could effect such limitation only by obviously vile and disreputable methods. So no one envisaged a policy of seeking to have just a reasonable number of children (by any method other than continence over sufficient periods) as a policy compatible with chastity. Indeed the very notion "a resonable number of children" could hardly be formulated compatibly with thinking at once decently and realistically. It had to be left to God what children one had.

With society becoming more and more contraceptive, the pressure felt by Catholic married people became great. The restriction of intercourse to infertile periods "for grave reasons" was offered to them as a recourse - at first in a rather gingerly way (as is intelligible in view of the mental background I have sketched) and then with increasing recommendation of it. For in this method the act of copulation was not itself adapted in any way so as to render it infertile, and so the condemnation of acts of contraceptive intercourse as somehow perverse and so as grave breaches of chastity, did not apply to this. All other methods, Catholics were very emphatically taught, were "against the natural law".

'Natural law' just means 'moral law'

Now I'd better pause a bit about this expression "against the natural law". We should notice it as a curiosity that in popular discussion there's usually more mention of "natural law" in connexion with the Catholic prohibition on contraception than in connexion with any other matters. One even hears people talk of "the argument from natural law". It's probable that there's a very strong association of words here: on the one hand through the contrast, "artificial"/"natural" and on the other through the terms "unnatural vice" or "sin against nature" which are labels for a particular range of sins against chastity; that is those acts which are wrong of their kind, which aren't wrong just from the circumstances that the persons aren't married: they're not doing what would be all right if they were married and had good motives - they're doing something really different. That's the range of sins against chastity which got this label "sin against nature".

In fact there's no greater connexion of "natural law" with the prohibition on contraception than with any other part of morality. Any type of wrong action is "against the natural law": stealing is, framing someone is, oppressing people is. "Natural law" is simply a way of speaking about the whole of morality, used by Catholic thinkers because they believe the general precepts of morality are *laws* promulgated by God our Creator in the enlightened human understanding when it is thinking in general terms about what are good and what are bad actions. That is to say, the discoveries of reflection and reasoning when we think straight about these things *are* God's legislation to us (whether we realise this or not).

In thinking about conduct we have to advert to laws of nature in another sense. That is, to very general and very well-known facts of nature, and also to ascertained scientific laws. For example, the resources of the earth have to be worked on to supply our needs and enhance our lives: this is a general and well-known fact of nature. Hence there needs to be control over resources by definite owners, be they tribes or states or cities or corporations or clubs or individual people: and this is the institution of property. Laws of nature in a scientific sense will affect the rules about control that it is reasonable to have. The type of installations we need if electricity is to be made available, for example, and the way they work, will be taken into account in framing the laws of the country or city about control of this resource. The institution of property has as its corollary the "law of nature" in the ethical sense, the sense of a law of morality, which forbids stealing. It's useful, very useful, to get clear about all this; it should help us to think and act justly and not to be too mad about property, too.

'Humanae Vitae'
- the only possible Christian teaching

It was in these various ways that the Pope spoke of natural laws in *Humanae Vitae* - the expression occurs in all these senses - and the topic of natural law in the ethical sense has not any greater relevance to contraception than to anything else. In particular, it is not because there is a *natural* law that something *artificial* is condemned.

The substantive, hard teaching of the Church which all Catholics were given up to 1964 was clear enough: all artificial methods of birth control were taught to be gravely wrong if, before, after, or during intercourse you do something intended to turn that intercourse into an infertile act if it would otherwise have been fertile.

At that time there had already been set up by Pope John in his lifetime a commission to enquire into these things. The commission consisted of economists, doctors and other lay people as well as theologians. Pope John, by the way, spoke of contraception just as damningly as his predecessor: it's a mere lie to suggest he favoured it. Pope Paul removed the matter from the competency of the Council and reserved to the Pope that new judgment on it which the modern situation and the new discoveries - above all, of oral contraceptives - made necessary.

From '64 onwards there was an immense amount of propaganda for the reversal of previous teaching. You will remember it. Then, with the whole world baying at him to change, the Pope acted as Peter. "Simon, Simon," Our Lord said to Peter, "Satan has wanted to have you to sift like wheat, but I have prayed for thee that thy faith should not fail: and thou, being once converted, strengthen thy brethren." Thus Paul confirmed the only doctrine which had ever appeared as the teaching of the Church on these things; and in so doing incurred the execration of the world.

But Athenagoras, the Ecumenical Patriarch, who has the primacy of the Orthodox Church, immediately spoke up and confirmed that this was Christian teaching, the only possible Christian teaching.

III. DISCUSSION OF THE TEACHING OF 'HUMANAE VITAE'

Its authority

Among those who hoped for a change, there was an instant reaction that the Pope's teaching was false, and was not authoritative because it lacked the formal character of an infallible document. Now as to that, the Pope was pretty solemnly confirming the only and constant teaching of the Church. The fact that an encyclical is not an infallible kind of document only shews that one argument for the truth of its teaching is lacking. It does not shew that the substantive hard message of this encyclical may perhaps be wrong - any more than the fact that memory of telephone numbers isn't the *sort* of thing that you *can't* be wrong about shews that you don't actually know your own telephone number.

A development of doctrine was needed ...

At this point one may hear the enquiry: "But isn't there room for development? Hasn't the situation changed?" And the answer to that is "Yes - there had to be development and there was." That, no doubt, was why Pope John thought a commission necessary and why it took the Pope four years to formulate the teaching. We have to remember that, as

Newman says, developments "which do but contradict and reverse the course of doctrine which has been developed before them, and out of which they spring, are certainly corrupt." No other development would have been a true one. But certainly the final condemnation of oral contraceptives *is* development - and so are some other points in the encyclical.

Development was necessary, partly because of the new physiological knowledge and the oral contraceptives and partly because of social changes, especially concerning women. The new knowledge, indeed, does give the best argument I know of that can be devised for allowing that contraceptives are after all permissible according to traditional Christian morals. The argument would run like this: There is not *much* ancient tradition condemning contraception as a distinct sin. The condemnations which you can find from earliest times were *almost* all of early abortion (called homicide) or of unnatural vice. But contraception, if it is an evil thing to do, is distinct from these, and so the question is really open. The authority of the teaching against it, so it is argued, is really only the authority of some recent papal encyclicals and of the pastoral practice in modern times.

... and 'Humanae Vitae' provided the only one which was faithful to the teaching but not absurd

Well, this argument has force only to prove the need for development, a need which was really there. It doesn't prove that it was open to the Pope to teach the permissibility of contraceptive intercourse. For how could he depart from the tradition forbidding unnatural vice on the one hand, and deliberate abortion, however early, on the other? On the other hand to say: "It's an evil practice if you do these things; but you may, without evil, practise such forms of contraception as are neither of them" - wouldn't that have been ridiculous? For example, "You shouldn't use withdrawal or a condom, or again an interuterine device. For the former involve you in acts of unnatural vice, and the latter is abortifacient in its manner of working. But you may after all use a douche or a cap or a sterilising pill." This would have been absurd teaching; nor have the innovators ever proposed it.

Contraception is not always a physical perversion

We have seen that the theological defence of the Church's teaching in modern times did not assimilate contraception to abortion but characterised it as a sort of perversion of the order of nature. The arguments about this were rather uneasy, because it is not in general wrong to interfere with natural processes. So long, however, as contraception took the form of monkeying around with the organs of intercourse or the act itself, there was some plausibility about the position because it really amounted to assimilating contraceptive intercourse to acts of unnatural vice (as some of them were), and so it was thought of.

So the intention is what is wrong

But this plausibility diminished with the invention of more and more sophisticated female contraceptives; it vanished away entirely with the invention of the contraceptive pill. For it was obvious that if a woman just happened to be in the physical state which such a contraceptive brings her into by art no theologian would have thought the fact, or the knowledge of it, or the use of the knowledge of it, straightaway made intercourse bad. Or, again, if a woman took an anovulant pill for a while to check dysmenorrhea no one would have thought this prohibited intercourse. So, clearly, it was the contraceptive intention that was bad, if contraceptive *intercourse* was: it is not that the sexual act in these circumstances is physically distorted. This had to be thought out, and it was thought out in the encyclical *Humanae Vitae*.

A confusion about intention ...

Here, however, people still feel intensely confused, because the intention where oral contraceptives are taken seems to be just the same as when intercourse is deliberately restricted to infertile periods. In one way this is true, and its truth is actually pointed out by *Humanae Vitae,* in a passage I will quote in a moment. But in another way it's not true.

... sorted out

The reason why people are confused about intention, and why they sometimes think there is no difference between contraceptive intercourse and the use of infertile times to avoid conception, is this: They don't notice the difference between "intention" when it means the intentionalness of the thing you're doing - that you're doing *this* on purpose - and when it means *a further* or *accompanying* intention *with* which you do the thing. For example, I make a table: that's an intentional action because I am doing just *that* on purpose. I have the *further* intention of, say, earning my living, doing my job *by* making the table. Contraceptive intercourse and intercourse using infertile times may be alike in respect of further intention, and these further intentions may be good, justified, excellent. This the Pope has noted. He sketched such a situation and said: "It cannot be denied that in both cases the married couple, for acceptable reasons," (for that's how he imagined the case) "are perfectly clear in their intention to avoid children and mean to secure that none will be born." This is a comment on the two things: contraceptive intercourse on the one hand and intercourse using infertile times on the other, for the sake of the limitation of the family.

But contraceptive intercourse is faulted, not on account of this further intention, but because of the kind of intentional action you are doing. The action is not left by you as the kind of act by which life is transmitted, but is purposely rendered infertile, and so changed to another sort of act altogether.

In considering an action, we need always to judge several things about ourselves. First: is the *sort* of act we contemplate doing something that it's all right to do? Second: are our further or surrounding intentions all right? Third: is the spirit in which we do it all right? Contraceptive intercourse fails on the first count; and to intend such an act is not to intend a marriage act at all, whether or no we're married. An act of ordinary intercourse in marriage at an infertile time, though, is a perfectly ordinary act of marital intercourse, and it will be bad, if it is bad, only on the second or third counts.

It may help you to see that the intentional act itself counts, as well as the further or accompanying intentions, if you think of an obvious example like forging a cheque to steal from somebody in order to get funds for a good purpose. The intentional action, presenting a cheque we've forged, is on the face of it a dishonest action, not to be vindicated by the good further intention.

Accepting contraceptive intercourse leaves no reasonable ground for rejecting perversion

If contraceptive intercourse is permissible, then what objection could there be after all to mutual masturbation, or copulation *in vase indebito,* sodomy, buggery[3], when normal copulation is impossible or inadvisable (or in any

---

[3] I should perhaps remark that I am using a *legal* term here - not indulging in bad language.

case, according to taste)? It can't be the mere pattern of bodily behaviour in which the stimulation is procured that makes all the difference! But if such things are all right, it becomes perfectly impossible to see anything wrong with homosexual intercourse, for example. I am not saying: if you think contraception all right you will do these other things; not at all. The habit of respectability persists and old prejudices die hard. But I am saying: you will have no solid reason against these things. You will have no answer to someone who proclaims, as many do, that they are good too. You cannot point to the known fact that Christianity drew people out of the pagan world, always saying no to these things. Because, if you are defending contraception, you will have rejected Christian tradition.

Difference between contraception and avoidance of infertile times

People quite alienated from this tradition are likely to see that my argument holds: that if contraceptive intercourse is all right then so are all forms of sexual activity. To them that is no argument against contraception; to their minds anything is permitted, so long as that's what people want to do. Well, Catholics, I think, are likely to know, or feel, that these other things are bad. Only, in the confusion of our time, they may fail to see that contraceptive intercourse, though much less of a deviation, and though it may not at all involve *physical* deviant acts, yet does fall under the same condemnation. For in contraceptive intercourse you intend to perform a sexual act which, if it has a chance of being fertile, you render infertile. *Qua* your intentional action, then, what you do *is* something intrinsically unapt for generation, and that is why it does fall under that condemnation. There's all the world of difference between this and the use of the "rhythm" method. For you use the rhythm method not just by having intercourse now, but by not having it next week, say; and not having it next week isn't something that does something to today's intercourse to turn it into an infertile act; today's intercourse *is* an ordinary act of intercourse, an ordinary marriage act. It's only if, in getting married, you proposed (like the Manichaeans) to confine intercourse to infertile periods, that you'd be falsifying marriage and entering a mere concubinage. Or if for mere love of ease and hatred of burdens you determined by this means never to have another child, you would then be dishonouring your marriage.

An analogy for this difference

We may be helped to see the distinction by thinking about the difference between sabotage and working-to-rule. Suppose a case where either course will have some typical aim of "industrial action" in view. Whether the aim is justified: that is the first question. But, given that it is justified, it's not all one how it is pursued.

If a man is working to rule, that does no doubt make *a* difference to the customary actions he performs in carrying out the work he does. It makes them also into actions in pursuit of such-and-such a policy. This is a matter of "further intention with which" he does what he does; admittedly it reflects back on his action in the way I have stated. That is to say: we judge that any end or policy gives a new characterisation of the means or of the detailed things done in executing it. All the same he is still, say, driving this vehicle to this place, which is part of his job.

If, however, he tries to sabotage his actions - he louses up a machine he is purporting to work, for example - that means that *qua* intentional action here and now his performance in "operating" the machine is *not* a doing of this part of his job. This holds quite without our having to point to the further intention (of industrial warfare) as reflecting back on his action. (And, *N.B.* it holds whether or not such sabotage is justified.)

Thus the distinction we make to shew that the "rhythm method" may be justified though contraceptive intercourse is not, is a distinction needed in other contexts too.

Why do the contraceptors rage?

The anger of the propagandists for contraception is indeed a proof that the limitation of conception by the "rhythm" method is hateful to their spirit. It's derided for not working. But it does work for many. And there were exclamations against the Pope for pressing medical experts to find out more, so that there could be certainty here. The anger I think speaks to an obscure recognition of the difference between ordinary intercourse with abstention at fertile times when you are justified in seeking not to conceive at present, and the practice of contraceptive intercourse.

Marriage - the goal of human sex acts

Biologically speaking, sexual intercourse is *the* reproductive act just as the organs are named generative organs from their role. Humanly speaking, the good and the point of a sexual act is marriage. Sexual acts that are not true marriage acts either are mere lasciviousness, or an Ersatz, an attempt to achieve that special unitedness which only a real commitment, marriage, can promise. For we don't invent marriage, as we may invent the terms of an association or club, any more than we invent human language. It is part of the creation of humanity and if we're lucky we find it available to us and can enter into it. If we are very unlucky we may live in a society that has wrecked or deformed this human thing.

This - that the good and the point of a sexual act is marriage - is why only what is capable of being a marriage act is natural sex. It's this that makes the division between straightforward fornication or adultery and the wickedness of the sins against nature and of contraceptive intercourse. Hence contraceptive intercourse within marriage is a graver offence *against chastity* than is straightforward fornication or adultery. For it is not even a proper act of intercourse, and *therefore* is not a true marriage act. To marry is not to enter into a pact of mutual complicity in no matter what sexual activity upon one another's bodies. (Why on earth should a ceremony like that of a wedding be needed or relevant if that's what's in question?) Marriage is a mutual commitment in which each side ceases to be autonomous, in various ways and also sexually: the sexual liberty in agreement together is great; here, so long as they are not immoderate so as to become the slaves of sensuality, nothing is shameful, if the complete acts - the ones involving ejaculation of the man's seed - that they engage in, are true and real marriage acts.

IV. THE VIRTUE OF CHASTITY

Every sex act is significant

That is how a Christian will understand his duty in relation to this small, but very important, part of married life. It's so important in marriage, and quite generally, simply because there just is no such thing as a casual, non-significant, sexual act. This in turn arises from the fact that sex concerns the transmission of human life. (Hence the picture that some have formed and even welcomed, of intercourse now, in this contraceptive day, losing its deep significance: becoming no more than a sort of extreme kiss, which it might be rather rude to refuse. But they forget, I think, the rewardless trouble of spirit associated with the sort of sexual activity which from its type is guaranteed sterile: the solitary or again the homosexual sort.)

There is no such thing as a casual, non-significant sexual act; everyone knows this. Contrast sex with eating - you're strolling along a lane, you see a mushroom on a bank as you pass by, you know about mushrooms, you pick it and you eat it quite casually - sex is never like that. That's why virtue in connection with eating is basically a matter only of the *pattern* of one's eating habits. But virtue in sex - chastity - is not *only* a matter of such a pattern, that is of its role in a pair of lives. A single sexual action can be bad even without regard to its context, its further intentions and its motives.

But sex is not a sacred action ...

Those who try to make room for sex as mere casual enjoyment pay the penalty: they become shallow. At any rate the talk that reflects and commends this attitude is always shallow. They dishonour their own bodies; holding cheap what is naturally connected with the origination of human life. There is an opposite extreme, which perhaps we shall see in our day: making sex a religious mystery. This Christians do not do. Despite some rather solemn nonsense that's talked this is obvious. We wouldn't, for example, make the sexual organs objects of a cultic veneration; or perform sexual acts as part of religious rituals; or prepare ourselves for sexual intercourse as for a sacrament.

... though the Christian view of sex ...

As often holds, there is here a Christian mean between two possible extremes. It is: never to change sexual actions so they are deprived of that character which makes sex so profoundly significant, so deep-going in human life. Hence we would not think of contraceptive intercourse as an exercise of *responsibility* in regard to sex! Responsibility involves keeping our sexual acts as that kind of act, and recognising that they are that kind of

act by engaging in them with good-hearted wisdom about
the getting of children. This is the standard of chastity for
a married Christian. But it should not be thought that it is
against wisdom for poor people willingly to have many
children. That is "the wisdom of the flesh, and it is
death"[4] (there's a lot of this death around at present).

... involves a mystical perception

Sexual acts are not sacred actions. But the perception of
the dishonour done to the body in treating them as the
casual satisfaction of desire is certainly a mystical
perception. I don't mean, in calling it a mystical
perception, that it's out of the ordinary. It's as ordinary as
the feeling for the respect due to a man's dead body: the
knowledge that a dead body isn't something to be put out
for the collectors of refuse to pick up. This, too, is
mystical; though it's as common as humanity.

Mystically-based virtues explained
by contrast with utilitarian virtue

I'm making this point because I want to draw a contrast
between two different types of virtue. Some virtues, like
honesty about property, and sobriety, are fundamentally
utilitarian in character. The very point of them is just the
obvious material well-ordering of human life that is

---

[4] Romans, ch.8 verse 6

promoted if people have these virtues. Some, though indeed profitable, are supra-utilitarian and hence mystical. You can argue truly enough, for example, that general respect for the prohibition on murder makes life more commodious. If people really respect the prohibition against murder life is pleasanter for all of us - but this argument is exceedingly comic. Because utility presupposes the *life* of those who are to be convenienced, and everybody perceives quite clearly that the wrong done in murder is done first and foremost to the victim, whose life is not inconvenienced, it just isn't there any more. He isn't there to complain; so the utilitarian argument has to be on behalf of the rest of us. Therefore, though true, it is highly comic and is not the foundation: the objection to murder is supra-utilitarian.

And so is the value of chastity. Not that this virtue isn't useful: it's highly useful. If Christian standards of chastity were widely observed the world would be enormously much happier. Our world, for example, is littered with deserted wives - partly through that fantastic con that went on for such a long time about how it was part of liberation for women to have dead easy divorce: amazing - these wives often struggling to bring up young children or abandoned to loneliness in middle age. And how many miseries and hang-ups are associated with loss of innocence in youth! What miserable messes people keep on making, to their own and others' grief, by dishonourable sexual relationships! The Devil has scored a great propaganda victory: everywhere it's suggested that the troubles connected with sex are all to do with frustration, with abstinence, with society's cruel and conventional disapproval. As if, if we could only do away with these things, it would be a happy and life-enhancing romp for everyone; and as if all who were chaste were unhappy, not only unhappy but hard-hearted and censorious and nasty. It fitted the temper of the times (this is a rather comic episode) when psychiatrists were asked to diagnose the unidentified Boston Strangler, they suggested he was a *sex-starved* individual. Ludicrous error! The idea lacks any foundation, that the people who are bent upon and who get a lot of sexual enjoyment are more gentle, merciful and kind than those who live in voluntary continence.

The trouble about the Christian standard of chastity is that it isn't and never has been generally lived by; *not* that it would be profitless if it were. Quite the contrary: it would be colossally productive of earthly happiness.

The world unconsciously shows its own mystical perception of the hatefulness of mere sensuality ...

All the same it is a virtue, not like temperance in eating and drinking, not like honesty about property, for these have a purely utilitarian justification. But it, like the respect for life, is a supra-utilitarian value, connected with the substance of life, and this is what comes out in the perception that the life of lust is one in which we dishonour our bodies. Implicitly, lasciviousness is over and over again treated as hateful, even by those who would dislike such an explicit judgment on it. Just listen, witness the scurrility when it's hinted at; disgust when it's portrayed as the stuff of life; shame when it's exposed, the leer of complicity when it's approved. You don't get these attitudes with everybody all of the time; but you do get them with everybody. (It's too much hard work to keep up the façade of the Playboy philosophy, according to which all this is just an unfortunate mistake, to be replaced by healthy-minded wholehearted praise of sexual fun.)

... thus bearing out the old teaching against sex "purely for pleasure"

And here we're in the region of that constant Christian teaching, which we've noticed, that intercourse "merely for the sake of pleasure" is wrong.

This can mislead and perturb. For when is intercourse purely for the sake of pleasure? Some have thought this must mean when it's not for the sake of getting a child. And so, I believe, I have been told, some Catholic women have actually feared the pleasure of orgasm and thought it wrong, or thought it wrong to look for it or allow oneself to respond to feelings of physical desire. But this is unreasonable and ungrateful to God. Copulation, like eating, is of itself a good kind of action: it preserves human existence. An individual act of eating or copulation, then, can be bad only because something about it or the circumstances of it make it bad. And all the pleasure specific to it will be just as good as *it* is.

We don't have to be trying to have babies ...

A severe morality holds that intercourse (and may hold this of eating, too) has something wrong about it if it is ever done except explicitly as being *required* for that preservation of human life which is what makes intercourse a good kind of action. But this involves thoroughly faulty moral psychology. God gave us our physical appetite, and its arousal without our calculation is part of the working of our sort of life. Given moderation and right circumstances, acts prompted by inclination can be taken in a general way to accomplish what makes them good in kind and there's no need for them to be individually necessary or useful for the end that makes them good kinds of action. Intercourse is a normal part of married life through the whole life of the partners in a marriage and is normally engaged in without any distinct purpose other than to have it, just *as* such a part of married life.

... to perform chaste marriage acts ...

Such acts will usually take place only when desire prompts, and desire is for intercourse as pleasurable; the pleasure, as Aristotle says, perfects the act. But that does not mean that it is done "purely for pleasure". For what that expression means is that sensuality is in command: but that one has intercourse when desire prompts and the desire is for pleasure, does not prove, does not mean, that sensuality is in command. One may rightly and reasonably be willing to respond to the promptings of desire. When that is so, the act is governed by a reasonable mind, even though no considering or reasoning is going on. The fact that one is thus having intercourse when, as one knows, there's nothing against it, makes it a good and a chaste marriage act and a rendering of the marriage debt.

... but sensuality should not hold sway

There is indeed such a thing in marriage as intercourse "purely for pleasure"; this is what the Christian tradition did condemn. Marks of it could be: immoderate pursuit of, or preoccupation with sexual pleasure; succumbing to desire against wisdom; insisting against *serious* reluctance of one's partner. In all these cases but the last both parties may of course be consenting. For human beings often tend to be disorderly and extreme in their sensuality. A simple test of whether one is so is this: could one do without for a few weeks or months in case of need? For anyone *may* be faced with a situation in which he ought to do

without; and he should watch that he does not get into a
state in which it is impossible for him.

The marriage debt

But we ought to remember also, what isn't always
remembered, that insensibility and unjustified abstention
is *also* a sin against moderation, and is a defrauding of
one's partner.

Well now, people raise the cry of "legalism" (one of the
regular accusations of the present day) against this idea
which I have taken from the old theologians of "rendering
what is owing", the giving the other person this part of
married life, which is owing. It embodies the one notion, I
would say, that is honest, truthful and quite general. People
would rather speak of the expression of mutual love. But
what do they mean by "love"? Do they mean "being in
love"? Do they mean a natural conjugal affection?

Either of these may be lacking or onesided. If a kind of
love cannot be commanded, we can't build our moral
theology of marriage on the presumption that it will be
present. Its absence is sad, but this sadness exists; it is very
common. We should avoid, I think, using the indicative
mood for what is really a commandment like the Scout
Law ("A Boy Scout is kind to animals" - it means a Boy
Scout ought to be kind to animals). For if we hear: "a
Christian couple grow in grace and love together" doesn't
the question arise "supposing they don't?" It clears the air

to substitute the bite of what is *clearly* a precept for the sweetness of a rosy picture. The command to a Christian couple is: "Grow in grace and love together." But a joint command can only be jointly obeyed. Suppose it isn't? Well, there remains the separate precept to each and in an irremediably unhappy marriage, one ought still to love the other, though not perhaps feeling the affection that cannot be commanded. Thus the notion of the "marriage debt" is a very necessary one, and it alone is realistic: because it makes no assumption as to the state of the affections.

Looking at the rightness of the marriage act like this will help in another way. It will prevent us from assuming that the pleasant affection which exists between a happy and congenial pair *is* the fulfilment of the precept of love. (It may after all only be a complacent hiving off together in a narrow love.) We ought absolutely not to give out a teaching which is flattering to the lucky, and irrelevant to the unhappy. Looked at carefully, too, such teaching is altogether too rigorist in a new direction. People who are not quite happily married, not lucky in their married life, but nevertheless have a loyalty to the bond, are not, therefore, bound to abstain from intercourse.

Marriage in the Christian vocation

The meaning of this teaching "not purely for pleasure" should, I think, have a great appeal for the Catholic thinking of today that is greatly concerned for the laity. We want to stress nowadays, that the one *vocation* that is spoken of in the New Testament is the calling of a Christian. All are called with the same calling. The life of monks and nuns and of celibate priesthood is a higher kind of life than that of the married, not because there are two grades of Christian, but because their form of life is one in which one has a greater chance of living according to truth and the laws of goodness; by their profession, those who take the vows of religion have set out to please God alone. But we lay people are not less called to the Christian life, in which the critical question is: "Where does the compass-needle of your mind and will point?" This is tested above all by our reactions when it costs or threatens to cost something to be a Christian. One should be glad if it does, rather than complain! If we will not let it cost anything; if we succumb to the threat of "losing our life", then our religion is indistinguishable from pure worldliness.

This is very far-reaching. But in the matter in hand, it means that we have got not to be the servants of our sensuality but to bring it into subjection. Thus, those who marry have, as we have the right to do, chosen a life in which, as St Paul drily says, "the husband aims to please his wife rather than the Lord, and the wife her husband, rather than the Lord" - but although we have chosen a life to please ourselves and one another, still we know we are called with that special calling, and are bound not to be conformed to the world, friendship to which is enmity to God.

Consequences for Christian communities

And so also we ought to help one another and have co-operative pools of help: help people who are stuck in family difficulties; and have practical resources in our parishes for one another's needs when we get into difficult patches.

The Church's witness

The teaching which I have rehearsed is indeed against the grain of the world, against the current of our time. But that, after all, is what the Church as teacher is for. The truths that are acceptable to a time - as, that we owe it as a debt of justice to provide out of our superfluity for the destitute and the starving - these will be proclaimed not only by the Church: the Church teaches *also* those truths that are hateful to the spirit of an age.